Stuck at the End of the Ice Age

by Luka Berman
illustrated by Arvis Stewart

 HOUGHTON MIFFLIN BOSTON

Sun, Surf, Sand — and Asphalt

When you hear the name "Los Angeles, California," what do you think of? Movie stars? Sunny beaches? Jam-packed freeways? Surfers? How about wooly mammoths?

Probably not that last one! But hard as it is to imagine, these prehistoric giants were once more common in California than convertibles. And you can still find them — or their fossils, at least — in the midst of the second-biggest city in the United States.

The La Brea Tar Pits in Los Angeles are home to one of the world's best Ice Age fossil sites. The fossils at La Brea reveal many details of life as it was between 10,000 and 40,000 years ago.

Model of a mastodon at the La Brea Tar Pits

What Are Tar Pits, Anyway?

Tar pits form when oil beneath the earth's surface seeps through cracks in the earth's crust. The light part of the oil evaporates, leaving behind shallow, sticky pools of tar, or asphalt. Tar pits began forming hundreds of thousands of years ago, and they still exist today. They're very rare, though, so don't worry about getting trapped in one!

In warm temperatures, from late spring to early fall, asphalt pools become soft, gooey, and treacherous. Animals and plants can become trapped in the sticky substance and die. A layer of asphalt about an inch and a half thick is enough to trap an animal the size of a cow.

During the last Ice Age, tar pits often formed near watering holes where animals went every day to drink. Dust and leaves covered the surface of the pits so they were well camouflaged, and animals had no idea what they were stepping into. Many animals got stuck in the sticky asphalt and could not escape.

After the trapped animals died, their remains were buried by layers of sand and silt that covered the pits during rainfall. Gradually, new asphalt pools formed, and more animals and plants were trapped. This continued for thousands of years.

Who Discovered the La Brea Fossils?

For a long time, no one knew what was hidden in the La Brea Tar Pits. Native Americans used the asphalt from the tar pits to glue and waterproof their baskets and canoes. Then Western settlers used the tar to make roofs. Spanish settlers named the pits *La Brea* — Spanish for "the tar."

In the 1800s, people began looking for valuable oil in the tar pits. Instead, they found bones. At first, no one thought much about the bones, figuring they belonged to cattle and horses that got stuck in the tar. But in 1875, Professor William Denton studied a tooth from the tar pits and discovered that it belonged to an extinct animal, the saber-toothed cat.

The Chumash, a tribe from southern California, tarred their canoes.

Then, in the early 1900s, scientists began major excavations at La Brea. The fossils they found were very well preserved. It didn't take long for scientists to recognize them as relics from the last Ice Age.

Today the George C. Page Museum of La Brea Discoveries, located beside the tar pits, displays more than three million La Brea fossils.

Why Are the Tar Pits So Important to Scientists?

When an animal or plant dies, its soft tissues usually decay or are eaten. Fossils form when bone or other hard parts are protected from decay. At La Brea, bones and other remains were protected by asphalt in the tar pits. The asphalt, which is waterproof, preserved the bones in perfect condition. It also helped keep skeletons in one piece.

The forefoot bones of a saber-toothed cat

In contrast, the bones discovered at most dinosaur digs are usually damaged, destroyed, or scattered.

Scientists have found more than a million bones at La Brea and have recorded more than 650 different kinds of animals so far, as well as about 140 species of plants. These fossils help paint a clearer picture of life in the Ice Age.

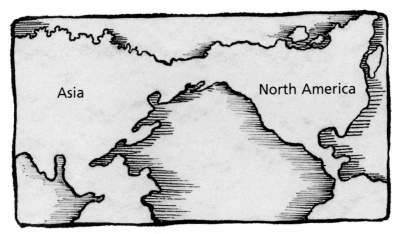

A land bridge brought animals from Asia to North America.

What Was Life Like 40,000 Years Ago?

Scientists believe the climate was cooler and wetter 40,000 years ago, based on the kinds of plant specimens they've found at La Brea. Many of the plant and animal fossils are similar or identical to species that still live in the area. But many of the larger animals found at La Brea are now extinct.

During the last Ice Age, a land bridge connected Asia and North America. Many animals crossed the land bridge and came down into what's now California.

The tar pits drew a rich diversity of Ice Age species.

The animals that crossed the land bridge included some you'd never expect to see in this country, such as camels! There were giant lions too, about the size of grizzly bears. Ground sloths as big as rhinoceroses were also common. (Their relatives today are about the size of raccoons.)

Among the most common fossils at La Brea are mammoths, wolves, and saber-toothed cats. Many mammoth fossils have been found at La Brea, but they have also been found in most other parts of the United States. The enormous Columbian mammoth (*Mammuthus columbi*) looked similar to an elephant, and its size was truly elephantine: it weighed as much as ten tons and stood almost fourteen feet high. Its tusks alone measured up to fourteen feet long! The American mastodon (*Mammut americanum*), in comparison, was a mere seven feet tall. It looked somewhat similar to mammoths and elephants, but it was actually only a distant relative.

Dire wolves, which were large ancestors of the grey wolf, are the most common fossils at La Brea. More than 3,600 of the animals have been found at the site. Scientists believe that dire wolves may have hunted in packs, which would account for so many getting stuck in the asphalt. Groups of wolves may have entered the tar pits together to feed on a creature that was already mired there.

The second-most common — but far and away most popular — fossils at La Brea belong to saber-toothed cats of the genus *Smilodon*. Hundreds of thousands of Smilodon bones have been found in the tar pits, representing thousands of animals. From these bones, scientists have constructed an amazingly detailed portrait of the Smilodon's appearance and lifestyle.

Often called saber-toothed tigers — probably because they looked a whole lot more ferocious than your average housecat — these animals actually weren't closely related to tigers. The Smilodon was about a foot shorter than a modern-day lion but almost twice as heavy. And unlike lions and tigers, which have long tails that help them balance while running, the Smilodon had a stubby tail.

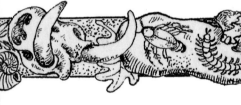

A Smilodon skeleton

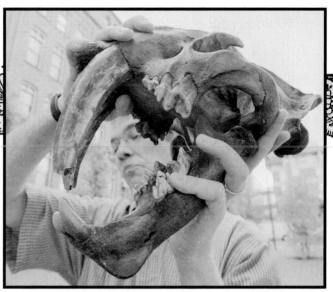

A million-year-old skull of a saber-toothed cat

These two details tell scientists that the Smilodon didn't spend much time chasing down its prey. Instead, it probably hid in tall grasses or bushes and pounced on unsuspecting prey. The Smilodon wasn't a champion runner, but one look at its famous "saber-teeth" — which could grow as long as eight inches — might convince you it was a champion biter. Not so, say scientists. Biting prey that way would probably result in a lot of broken saber-teeth — but very few have been found among the La Brea fossils. Therefore, scientists suspect that the Smilodon used its enormous teeth like knives to stab its prey rather than grab and bite them.

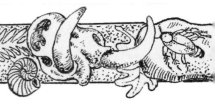

Excavators digging up
particles at La Brea

Despite its uncuddly personality — and the fact that it lived all over North and South America — Smilodon is so beloved by visitors to La Brea that it has been named California's state fossil. Its role as family pet on *The Flintstones* may have given it an unfair advantage over the dire wolf.

Not all the fossils found at La Brea are big and extinct. Scientists have also found tiny or microscopic plant remains such as pollen, seeds, leaves, and wood. And there are clam and snail shells, insects and spiders, fish, frogs, salamanders and toads, snakes, lizards, turtles, and birds — in all, more than 565 species. Many of the plant and small animal species are still found in southern California, although some no longer live there because the area is now so crowded with people, buildings, and freeways.

Why Were Some Animals Trapped More Often Than Others?

Very few nocturnal animals were trapped in the asphalt at La Brea. This is because the asphalt in the tar pits hardened on cool nights, so animals that were active only at night didn't get trapped.

Scientists were more puzzled to find that 90 percent of the fossils at La Brea belong to carnivorous (meat-eating) animals. In the normal food chain, herbivores (plant eaters) outnumber carnivores by as much as 200 to 1. One theory may explain why so many carnivores got trapped at La Brea. If a herbivore got stuck in the tar, it probably attracted several hungry meat-eaters, which would also get trapped. For example, a horse (a herbivore) might be chased into a tar pit and become trapped. Then several saber-toothed cats and dire wolves (all carnivores) might have gone after the horse and become trapped themselves.

Volunteers excavate around the bones of trapped carnivores.

Animals probably didn't get trapped in the tar pits every day. But even if only ten large mammals got stuck in the asphalt every ten years, that would be enough to account for the millions of bones discovered at La Brea.

Why No Dinosaurs?

Believe it or not, wooly mammoths and saber-toothed cats are very modern animals compared to dinosaurs. Dinosaurs became extinct about 65 million years before the La Brea Tar Pits even began to form!

GEOLOGIC TIME CHART

Cenozoic Era
63 million years ago to present

Mesozoic Era
240 to 63 million years ago

Paleozoic Era
570 to 240 million years ago

Why Are So Many Ice Age Animals Extinct?

No animal species became extinct simply by walking into the tar pits. The number of fossils found in La Brea — even those from the most commonly found animal, the dire wolf — represent only a tiny fraction of each animal's total population during the last Ice Age.

So if all the animals didn't sink into the asphalt, what became of them?

Scientists are still trying to figure that out. Nearly 40 percent of all the species represented at La Brea, most of them large mammals, became extinct between 11,000 and 8,000 years ago, and no one is sure why. But there are several theories. Climatic changes at the end of the last Ice Age may have been dramatic enough to kill off or alter the vegetation that many herbivores ate. If so, the herbivores would have slowly starved. In turn, the carnivores that subsisted on the herbivores would have starved.

Humans are another possible culprit. Homo sapiens arrived in North America before many of the large mammals died off. One controversial theory claims that people hunted some of the animals to extinction. Scientists who believe this theory point out that species on several continents became extinct at around the same time that humans arrived. But it's not clear whether there were sufficient numbers of humans, with sufficient means, to kill off entire species.

A third possibility is that disease wiped out many species. Or perhaps all three factors — climatic change, human intervention, and disease — played a role. Maybe the fossils at La Brea will help reveal the answer.

Are Scientists Still Finding Fossils at La Brea?

Every year, about 1,000 new bones are excavated from the tar pits. Teams of scientists work in one part of a pit at a time, carefully noting the location and position of each fossil they find. Then they remove, clean, examine, identify, and document each bone. Visitors to La Brea can see the discoveries as they take place.

You might say La Brea is a bottomless pit of fossils — and a mammoth natural wonder!

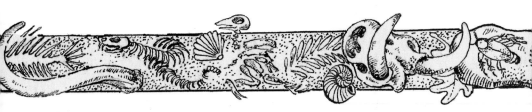